Hypnosis

IIII|II||III|III|II|III|II|III|IIII
I0413357

A to Z

Hypnotic Words & Phrases

This book is dedicated to my wife Georgina

&

Aaron, Adam, Aidan

My three sons

For supporting me throughout the writing of this book

HOW TO USE THIS BOOK

Set out in the style of a dictionary it is intended to be used by the reader as a quick reference guide as to complement mine and indeed any other hypnosis books.

Identifying specific issues especially for the beginner without the need to trawl page after page or keep dozens of bookmarks.

As long as you can remember the words or phrases you can go straight to the relevant page and refresh your memory. This will be an invaluable tool to support your learning and way beyond.

Written in plain English with a minimum of technocratic wording it is designed to be an aid not a hindrance. So many dictionary style books need an additional thesaurus in order to decipher the simplest of descriptions this book is laid out specifically to avoid that.

Read from cover to cover or as and when needed. This book will be a trusted companion for any hypnotist, from beginner to master.

CONTENTS

THE A's

AARON SCALE

Commonly used trance depth measurement. This scale has 6 levels and uses different hypnotic phenomena to gauge depth of the scale.

Stage 1. Hypnoidal, this is very light similar to the daydream state we all experience on a daily basis. At this stage it is possible to control small muscle groups such as the eyelids. Hypnoidal states can also be induced as a response to trauma. For example people involved in car accidents will often act as if in a trance. It is part of the natural defence mechanisms built into all of us.

Stage 2. This might be considered a medium stage of hypnosis large muscle groups can be controlled such as arm rigidity (catalepsy). The critical factor has been bypassed.

Stage 3. Medium to deep. Now we can control the entire body make it feel whatever is suggested. Hot, cold even glove analgesia.

Stage 4. Deep, subjects can be made to forget names, numbers, addresses etc.

Stage 5. The threshold of somnambulism. We can achieve positive hallucinations.

Stage 6. Somnambulism. Negative hallucinations can be induced.

ABREACTION

The expression and consequent release of a previously repressed emotion, achieved through reliving the experience that caused it.

It often happens when the subject is regressed back to a time in their lives when there was a dramatic incident of some description. Abreactions can be used as part of the therapeutic process These revivications of the causative event along with understanding it and finally releasing of the repression will free the subject of the symptom

On stage however they happen inadvertently and are most undesirable

To deal with an abreaction simply say the following.

Leave that memory behind as you come back to the here and now.

To safeguard against abreactions use the expression 'as if', so you would say something like, 'it's as if you were six years old' instead of 'imagine you are six years old'. It is a subtle but important difference.

Signs of abreaction.

Unexpected facial expressions incongruent to the suggestions being made

Frowning

Contortions of the face which reflect inner turmoil

Weeping

Short sharp intakes of breath

Hand and arm movements inconsistent with the expected

ABNORMAL

Not normal. Can refer to phobic reactions and the like where the level of reaction to the stimulus is unusual compare to what might be normally expected

ACCEPTANCE

Acknowledgement of the issue by a subject. Also used in reference to accepting a causative event in therapy

ADDICTIONS

This is a condition whereby a person is menta.ly and physically over dependent on a substance. Addiction can be treated with hypnotherapy. There may be some quite dangerous side effects during withdrawal and so this must always be done in conjunction with other medical health workers such as a GP.

ADVERTISING

The advertising world is the master of waking hypnosis and uses it to influence all of us all the time. It is fascinating that mediums using cold reading and hypnotic techniques in order to bring comfort and peace to those that believe in such things are called Charlatan's. While on the other hand a fast food company which sells nutritionally worthless burgers and such, high in all that is bad for us can advertise on TV between end cf school hours and the watershed. SEE COVERT, SUBLIMINALS, OVERLOAD.

AFFECT

Making a difference to something. This is the fundamentally what we do with hypnosis, we use it to affect the subject

AFFIRMATION

Used as part of the ego strengthening or confidence building process positive affirmation is given to the subject. Statements such as. You are a talented person capable of achieving anything you set out to do. These statements have a very powerful and positive effect on the subconscious.

AGE PROGRESSION

Going forward in time. Used in timeline therapy, to help subjects visualise themselves in the future having made positive changes today.

AGE REGRESSION

The process of taking a subject back to earlier times in their life. This is a popular method of attempting to find the beginning or start of a particular problem, the causative event often phobias.

ALPHA

A state of deep relaxation where brainwave cycles are between 7.5 and 14 Hz.

ALLERGY

An allergy is when a person is overly sensitive to what would be considered a normal substance to most. Use extreme caution if attempting to use hypnotherapy as part of any treatment for an allergy. Any such treatment must be carried out alongside medical health workers such as a GP.

ALTERED STATE

Hypnosis or the trance state itself is often described as an altered state. It is a shift in the usual state of consciousness to another.

AMNESIA

Memory loss. We can induce memory loss in a subject quite easily. Giving amnesia to a subject or subjects during a performance is very popular due to its hilarity. The stage volunteer can be made to forget just about anything. Also we use amnesia as part of depth testing. Once we are able to induce amnesia we can be sure that the subject has reached medium to deep level of trance. Amnesia can also be used to have a subject forget the actual content of a session. Especially when post hypnotics are used.

AMBIGUOUS

Hypnotic language should for the most part be ambiguous. If we are too specific sometimes this can be distracting to the subject. Also when relying on the double bind ambiguity is a useful tool.

ANAL

One of the so called character types. Anal characters develop awareness between the ages of two and five. This creates the situation where subconscious reactions to outside stimuli become protective. They are said to be materialistic, suspicious, intolerant and mean spirited. Anal types become power obsessive and lack the ability to empathise.

ANALYTICAL

A personality type. Someone who is most comfortable trying to reason and understand what is going on. Analytical types also like to keep their minds busy all the time. It can make them a challenge to hypnotise.

ANCHOR

A physical act used to trigger an event. Most common is the ring of confidence for subjects wh need a boost in self esteem and have very little confidence. This is the touch ng of the thumb and forefinger together to form a circle. When this is done a preset action occurs.

During the therapy session we would have the subject remember a time when they felt very confident then have them amplify that feeling to a point where they are experiencir g a high degree of confidence. Then at that point we tell the subject to touch the finger and thumb together and also give a post hypnotic suggestion that whenever they do this they will re-experience the feelings of high confidence they are currently feeling.

ANALGESIA

This is the loss of sensation of pain. Suggestions are given that an area of the body has complete loss of feeling and that no matter what happens there will be no sensation of pain. The subject is then tested, the hypnotist will typically pinch them or even prick them with a needle. Analgesia in a subject is a good indicator that the deeper stages of hypnosis have been achieved.

Hypnotically induced analgesia has been used in childbirth, dentistry and even major surgery!

ANAMNESIS

Recalling of memories. In trance particularly during analytical therapy techniques using regression a heightened ability to recall past events is induced in order to discover the symptom causing event.

ANIMAL MAGNETISM

This is what Meser called hypnotism when he first discovered and induced trance states. The use of magnets also contributed to this term.

ANNIVERSARY REACTION

A symptom which displays itself on the anniversary of the initiating event. Subjects have exactly the same physical and or emotional symptoms on the same date every year. Someone having broken an arm on a particular day will experience aches and pains in that same arm on the same day each year thereafter.

ANXIETY

A negative emotional state. A fear of the unknown Anxiety is the symptom to the repressed event.

ANXIETY ATTACK

People having felt the effects of anxiety attacks describe a feeling of being distressed and apprehensive. Feelings of impending doom and a general fear are also how people can feel. It is important to distinguish feelings of anxiety from genuine fear. Fear is a genuine response to a stimulus which presents danger of some sort. Anxiety is objectless. Stress related problems can be attributed to anxiety.

Common signs of anxiety attacks are:

Physical shaking

Frozen to the spot

Stomach ache

Increased heart rate

Increase in breathing

Hot flush

Tingling sensations

And many more

ARM LOCK

A common catalepsy procedure used in hypnosis. See catalepsy.

ARM LEVITATION

Used as a suggestibility test as initial induction as well as a trance depth test. Suggestions are given that the arm is becoming increasingly lighter until the subject responds. When used for suggestibility test it is also a very good convincer. As a trance depth test it is an indicator of light to medium trance. Can be used as the beginnings of an induction too. Once the levitation occurs these feelings are transferred into feelings of weight and depth and the entire body is then included.

ASSESS

Making judgments with regard to subjects suitability for hypnotherapy or how best to deal with their particular issue. Good assessments save time and improve a subjects experience. Also risk assessments. Taking into consideration potential dangers and or hazards. Making reasonable judgments as to the likely hood of the occurrence of these also the severity of the outcome. Once all factors are considered the risk is determined.

AS IF

A very common and powerful expression. Whenever describing something to a subject if we use the term 'as if' we are using ambiguity as well as specifics. It's a way of giving the subconscious some wiggle room. If you were to suggest something to a subject in a very specific term the unconscious might be alerted and become less cooperative with the trance process.

Suppose you had a volunteer on stage who is a fanatic about guitar playing. He can play and he knows that he himself is a mediocre guitar player. Also as a fan he has definite views about who the great guitar players in the world are. You suggest to this subject that he is the greatest guitar player in the world. His beliefs about a subject in which he is very knowledgeable will not allow this falsehood. His critical factor starts to stir and a sort of de-convincing process starts lightning or even ending the trance..

Now if the same suggestion is reframed as. 'It's as if you are the the greatest guitar player in the world'. Straight away he' s jumping around the stage playing air guitar. You see the wiggle room, in his mind now it can be as if he is Carlos Santana or he can be like Eric Clapton. You have allowed him to cooperate with you and create a convincer for the next 'as if'.

ASSOCIATION

A link between two or more things. Such as an association between a trigger and a response. An example of this might be 'whenever I cough you will say the word peanuts'. The same thing is happening between stimulus and symptom only this is , in the case of phobias etc, a negative association.

ASSUME HYPNOSIS

Once you start the process of hypnotising assume hypnosis will and is taking place. This helps with your own confidence and with convincing the subject.

ASTRAL PROJECTION

A supposed out of body experience where the astral body leaves the physical body. This kind of experience is often induced by hypnotists as part of a past life regretion session. Subjects are taken out of their physical body and then travel back through time to a former life.

ATTENTION

This means taking notice of something. This is a conscious activity. Focussing the subjects attention is fundamental to helping induce trance.

Alsoattention is what must be paid the hypnotist, attention to what is happening at all times during the session.

ATTITUDE CHANGE

One of the outcomes expected when hypnosis is employed. The subject starts with a preconception regarding an idea when the subject accepts a new concept we have acheived a change of attitude. We use this with therapies like smoking cessation. It is not enough to just have the subject give up the dreaded weed. We should be changing their attitude toward all aspects of smoking to ensure lasting success.

AUDITORY TYPES

People who primarily 'think' in terms of sound. When thinking internally they 'converse' with themselves. Their use of memory is audio based too. They listen to their minds ear as apposed to seeing with their minds eye which is how visual types internalise. Also auditory types use language which reflects this. They might confirm information by saying something like 'I hear what you are getting at'.

AUTOHYPNOSIS

Another term for the art of self hypnosis. The operator and the subject is the same person. Hypnosis is self induced. Progressive relaxation is the chosen method usually however those that are well practiced can self hypnotise very quickly. In fact meditation may be a better term for this kind of activity. It is also widely believed that all hypnosis is self hypnosis and that hypnotists are merely guides for the subject.

AUTOMATIC WRITTING

Writing under hypnosis with no conscious effort or thought. Usually associated with the spiritualist world more than therapy.

AUTONOMIC NERVOUS SYSTEM

The part of the nervous system responsible for the automatic regulation of the basic life processes. Heart beat breathing etc. This process is controlled by the subconscious mind.

AUTO SUGGESTION

The process of making changes within oneself by means of self suggesting. Repetition of self affirming sayings is the most common. Neurolinguistic programming at its most fundamental. The repetition of self affirming statements leads to positive change.6

AVERSION THERAPY

This is a therapy which attempts to link an unpleasant experience with a particular behaviour. For example associating the act of smoking with a foul taste. For example;

Each time you light a cigarette your mouth will fill with the taste of faeces... The taste will seem to be so real that you may even become nauseas.

Not very element but can be effective in certain cases.

AWAKE

The normal state of consciousness.

AWAKEN

To bring someone back out of a trance state. Also known as emergence or trance termination

AWARENESS

The subjective state of being conscious.

AWE

Surprise and fear is how most describe the emotion 'awe'. Hypnotist rely on this in potential subjects it in turn creates expectation and belief that something is going to take place they convince themselves that they are going to be hypnotised.

The proof of this is that the more well known or 'famous' a hypnotist the easier it is for him to hypnotise people. You see his reputation precedes him the people he interacts with are in awe of his previously proven work. Add to this the almost mystical aura surrounding some of these people and presto. There is a case to be heard that once in the presense of these hpnotists they are already in a mild state of trance.

THE B's

BARNUM STATEMENTS

Statements which are quite vague but seem to be specific to any individual they are directed at. Double binds are often used in part of the statement in order ensure that some part of the contact will seem a truism to just about anyone. Widely used as part of cold reading especially toward the beginning in order to hone in on the most susceptible.

BANDER & GRINDLER

After studying the work of Milton Erickson these two psychologists created what is known as NLP (neuro-linguistic programming). They used the link between the nervous system language and behaviour. NLP is the ability to use language to program ourselves and others. It is a form of waking hypnosis.

BASELINE

A starting point from which all other readings are taken. By observing and establishing a baseline of behavior, expressions and breathing etc. the hypnotist can more easily observe change to stimuli.

BECAUSE

One of the hypnotic power words. When used correctly it implies that since one thing is so the next will be too. Things are happening because the hypnotist says so.

BEGINNING

The start. From the therapeutic point of view all phobias have a beginning. If we find the beginning and adjust the thinking the phobia no longer exists.

The beginning of hypnosis starts with first contact, building expectancy and belief as well as constantly convincing

BEHAVIOUR

Psychologists are still arguing the true definition of the word behaviour. From the hypnotists point it is less of an issue. In a therapy room we are generally presented with subjects that would like to change something about themselves. In their view they want to change a negative behaviour. On stage we generally are trying to create strange and comedic behaviors.

BELIEF

Belief is a very important aspect in hypnosis for both the hypnotist and the subject. For the hypnotist absolute belief in his abilities is essential for his success. The subject must believe also that whatever the hypnotist says is going to happen will happen.

A good hypnotist will create belief in the subject by conveying his confidence and his knowledge of hypnotism to the potential subject, also by using convincers and suggestibility tests. Eventually his reputation alone will do most of the work for him.

BELIEF SYSTEMS

These are the beliefs we have, often handed down, which may or may not be correct. But they are so deeply ingrained in our subconscious we believe them even if there is empirical proof to the contrary. In therapy it is widely believed that we are our parenting. Belief systems can often be a destructive influence in our everyday life.

'What someone doesn't know will not hurt them'. This is a negative belief, in a relationship this is a damaging belief, even a person consciously understanding that this is an unhealthy attitude will not be able to stop acting upon it.

BETA

The normal waking state where brainwave cycles are between 14 and 40 Hz.

BIOFEEDBACK LOOP

This tool is essential to the hypnotist. It is the skill of observing the physical state of the subject and feeding this information back in such a way as to imply that it is in fact the suggestion which came first. An example is; you notice that the subjects eyes flutter slightly and you say ' that's right...well done...as your eyelids become heavier you notice that they may flutter slightly.... Etc.

Also used in cold reading ; the reader throws out a statement, or many statements in quick succession. The subject makes a small micro expression at the mention of a name or place. The reader sees this give away that they have struck a chord and continues down this path becoming more specific all the time.

The ultimate feedback loop is the nodding head question referred to later in this book.

BODY LANGUAGE

Part of the non verbal communication family. The body posture along with body movement and facial expression is present in all of us all of the time. From the unconscious shuffling of feet to the conscious posing. To be a great hypnotist you need to have an excellent understanding of body language.

BREATHING

Although this is a natural reoccurring action, it is a very useful tool which hypnotists employ as part of relaxation, convincers, rapport building and trance ididentification.

Breathing and relaxation. When we breath out or exhale our body has a natural tendency to relax this is especially true if we have taken a deeper than usual breath and if we exhale through our mouths. It is because when we take a deep breath as we fill our lungs our body tends to rise up, so of course on exhaling the body seems to 'drop' further than usual, accompany this with hypnotic verbal encouragement and we can dramatically increase the feeling of relaxation. Also when we exhale through our mouth the air passes across thousands of nerve endings causing intense comforting feelings at a limbic level.

Breathing and rapport. The hypnotist can use breathing as part of the rapport building process. Matching breathing pattern is usually the first step in matching mirroring and leading. Indead whenever suggestions relating to breathing are made the hypnotist must non verbally do what he is suggesting.

Breathing in trance identification. Shallower than normal breathing is a classic sign of trance. As for it being used as a convincer, as is mentioned several times throughout this book, everything is a convincer.

Short sharp shallow breaths during hypnosis may be signs of abreaction.

BRAID

In the mid 19th century the Scottish doctor James Braid invented the term 'hypnosis' from the Greek word for sleep, 'Hypnos'. He later discovered that trance and the trance phenomena catalepsy, amnesia etc could be induced without actual sleep. By the time he realised his mistake and attempted to change the name of hypnosis to monoideism it was too late since the term hypnosis had become widely accepted.

BRAIN

The physical organ with which associate thinking, consciousness, subconscious and all. Not to be confused with the 'mind' where the conscious, unconscious and subconscious actually reside.

BRAIN WASHING

This is in no way linked to hypnosis in the everyday sense. It means to change the attitude of a person toward their basic beliefs. It takes a great deal of time and usually involves sensory deprivation and the like. Bringing a person to the brink of madness making them hyper suggestible and then 'saving' them with commands.

BRAINWAVES

These are measured in cycles per second. In scientific hypnosis they are the measuring scale for hypnotic trance states. They are Beta, Alpha, Theta and Delta. The frequency ranges from about 40Hz which is the normal waking state (Beta) right down to 0.5 Hz deep sleep (Delta). Between are Deep relaxation between 7.5 and 14 Hz (Alpha) and meditative sleep between 4 and 7.5 Hz (Theta).

BREUER

We can thank Joseph Breuer for the concept of regression and symptom removal using analytical therapy. He discovered that his patients could remember repressed events and once these events were confronted and understood symptoms disappeared.

THE C's

CADENCE

The rhythm with which we speak, usually a sort of soothing singsong almost poetic quality, especially in therapy. Can often mean the tapering off of words at the end of a spoken sentence, this can imply depth to the subconscious.

CALM

Everything about the hypnotist should be calm. He should exude confidence. In the therapy too calmness keeps everything in perspective. The exception to this rule is when we want to create excitement, on stage for instance, then we might be loud and colourful with our language and movement in order to encourage the acceptance of both the emotional and physical content of a particular sketch.

CATALEPSY

Rigidity of a part or the body. Also means that a part of the body is unable to move once set in position. Examples of catalepsy in hypnosis are things like eye catalepsy, this is slightly misleading since in reality it is eye lid catalepsy. Eye catalepsy is a very good all round tool used in suggestibility testing, as a convincer, for deepening and for depth testing.

CAUSE

The root of an issue usually the initial event or trauma leading to the symptom. Whenever dealing with phobias and the like it is preferable to find the cause. Failing to identifying the cause may result in symptom replacement

CAUSATIVE EVENT

The initial event which started the process of stimuli results in a symptom. We could say that when it comes to symptoms, everything has a beginning and the beginning would be the causative event.

CATHARSIS

Having a good reaction to the hypnotic experience. The opposite of an abreaction

CHANGE

This is the purpose of hypnosis. On stage or street where the purpose is to entertain we require temporary change. In therapy its a lot different the purpose here is to cause permanent positive change. Often these changes may transform a subjects life completely.

CHARACTER TYPES

This is one of the theories postulated by Sigmund Freud. He believed that humans can be categorised as belonging to one of three basic character types. ANAL, ORAL, GENITAL. It is possible for individuals to display charecteristics of all three types in varying degrees.

CHARCOT

Jean Martin Charcot a 19th century neurologist, primarily interested in hysteria. He claimed that only the hysterical could be hypnotised. He was responsible for the first scaling of hypnotic depths. He claimed there were three stages; lethargy, catalepsy and somnambulism.

COGNITIVE DISSONANCE

The conflict between a personal belief and observations of the outside world leading to a distortion of the perceived reality instead of changing the belief.

COGNITIVE SYSTEM

The conscious processes such as reasoning and logic. Thinking

COLD READING

This is a technique used by mediums and mentalists to create the illusion of having phsycic powers. It is the reading of body language, expressions and micro expressions. Usually the reader will make a few barnum statements then read the biofeedback signs to make more personal statements. Eventually seeming to be able to read minds.

COMPOUNDING

In hypnosis we use a technique called compounding in order to reinforce suggestions. We repeat the instructions but also vary the wording slighty, we do this over and over during therapy quite literally compounding the idea into the subconscious mind. Not to be confused with repetition.

COMPULSIONS

Feeling the need to repeatedly perform some task or another without seemingly being able to control the urge. Compulsions as with other negative behaviours are simply symptoms.

CONCENTRATION

This is required of the subject. Full concentration is needed in order that they do exactly as they are directed. The concentration is needed also in order for them to notice the changes fully, not only in their minds but also physiologically. See (Imagination/ Concentration/ Intelligence)

CONVERSION

A shift from one state to another. For examp.e changing an unhealthy habit for a healthy one.

COMPLETE COMPLIANCE

The complete compliance suggestion is a very elegent tool which should be used on all subjects. It ensures that the subject will follow suggestions. It can be used at any time after initial induction. Example of the sort of wording used in complete compliance;

From this point forward all the time you are here...

You will find that every suggestion I put to you...

Will become your complete and instant reality

No matter how strange the suggestion may seem...

Just as your eyes remained closed...

When I said they would...

And because i said your arm would be locked...

It was in fact locked...

Whatever I suggest will be your reality...

Whatever I say you can see...

You will see...

Whatever I say you can feel...

You will feel...

Whatever I say you can hear...

You will hear...

You will carry out every suggestion instantly and faithfully...

Nod your head when you understand.

COMPLIANCE

A requirement by the subject at all times during hypnosis. Since you are the guide the subject must comply with your instructions. Each time the subject complies with a suggestion they become more likely to comply with the next (see convincers).

CONDITIONED RESPONSE

A particular response to given trigger.

CONDITIONING

Conditioning, as with most things hypnotic, is multilayered, first to get them ready for the hypnotic experience good pretalk and use of convinces. Secondly each time someore enters trance they become better at it, it is a skill. Also by giving post hypnotic suggestions that they will reenter trance at a later time when they receive a certain trigger.

CONFIDENCE

For a successful hypnotist this is probably the most important quality. You must have absolute confidence in every aspect. Yourself, your abilities and that you will achieve whatever it is you set out to do. Without it you are doomec.

You must also create confidence in the subjects mind. First they must be confident in your abilities as a hypnotist and also confidence that they will achieve their goals, especially in therapy.

CONFUSION

One of the methods used to induce hypnosis.

CONGRUENCE

Sometimes referred to as genuineness. In the therapy room it is important that we have congruence betweer our body language and what we are saying. Clients will know if you are not genuine

CONSCIOUS

The part of the mind which deals with the here and now. The conscious mind is analytical and does the evaluating of information as it is received. It cross references with the subconscious mind for information stored. The conscious is only capable of holding one thought at a time.

CONTROL

One of the great myths and misconceptions. The hypnotist cannot control another person. A subject cannot be made to do anything that they are fundementaly apposed to. The idea that you can turn a perfectly docile human being into an assassin or mass murderer is nonsense.

CONVINCERS

The more a subject is convinced the are hypnotised or that they will follow a suggestion made bythe hypnotist then tne more they become hypnotised or the more suggestible they become. As they follow an instruction so they become more convinced that they will follow the next.

COOPERATION

The subject must at all times cooperate with your suggestions and your guidance. This should be made clear very early on in the proceedings. On stage any signs of non cooperation by a subject should be dealt with straight way, usually by politely sending them back to their seat. Non cooperating subjects are spoilers! Any sign of non cooperation in therapy may signify nervousness and this should also be dealt with immediately, usually further interview and better pretalk is all that is required.

COUE

Emile Coue lived in the late eighteenth and early nineteenth centuries. He was the father of suggestion. He discovered the placebo effect and understood that positive suggestion brings about positive change. When we put hypnosis together with cous methods and 'laws' we have hypnotherapy.

COUE'S LAW OF REVERSED EFFECT

Coue's law of reverse effect states that when the conscious is in conflict with the imagination the imagination will always win. The classic example for this is to tell someone to not think of a pink elephant. They consciously try not to think of a pink elephant but immediately imagine one.

COUNCELLING

A broad term for shadowing and shepherding an individual whilst they undergo personal change. This involves listening, evaluating and advising. Truly excellent hypnotherapists are also good councilors.

COUNTER TRANSFERENCE

The hynotherapists emotional involvement in the therapeutic interaction. Usually due to the rapport which exists between the two.

COUNTING

Using counting is part of the bread and butter language patterns used by hypnotists. Counting down is used as part of deepeners obviously encouraging depth. Count up to encourage upward motions often right up to trance termination. Also used in fractioning and as triggers.

COVERT

Covert hypnosis is the realm of the NLP'ers. The use or language in patterns to influence others, it is of course very possible to do this. Covert hypnosis is used every day in advertising. Especially TV advertising where a variety of senses are overloaded.

The conscious mind can only focus or concentrate on one thing at a time. It is easy to overload the conscious and when we do that who knows what might happen. SEE OVERLOAD.

CRIMINAL SUGGESTION

Another misconception, you cannot force a person to carry out a criminal act using hypnosis. No one can be forced to act in a way which is contrary to their beliefs. For a person to carry out a criminal act they must be predisposed in this direction already.

CRITICAL FACTOR

This is the term often given to the gatekeeper of the mind. It is there to protect us. This is the part of the mind we as hypnotherapists need to bypass in order to access the subconscious.

CURE

The repair of an organism. Its return to normal healthy functioning. Beware that hypnotherapy is not curring it is a process of re-aligning or re-educating the subconscious actions to the conscious desire.

THE D's

DANGERS OF HYPNOTISM

The only dangers associated with hypnotism are the misconceptions surrounding hypnosis itself. Thanks to the popular press and TV fiction. Hypnosis is a completely safe and natural state.

DAY DREAM

The state which we all experience several times a day. It is in fact the first stages of hypnosis. The brain creates vivid images in the minds eye whilst awake, a person may be more than usually suggestible during daydreaming.

DEBRIEF

A short talk after a hypnosis session of any kind. After a stage or street performance it may simply be a few questions in order to establish the subjects are in fine fettle. A post therapy debrief should cover what has been achieved, how the subject feels and future plans. Following a stage or street session the operator should make himself available to the subjects for a reasonable amount of time afterwards in case of any issues. The hypnotism act 1952 specifically states that the hypnotist should be available for thirty minutes after a show.

DEFENDANCE

To justify ones actions. A phenomena present in many subjects when acting out a suggestion, they maintain that whatever happened was by their own choice. Sometimes on stage this will happen even after the most ridiculous activity has taken place.

DEEPENERS

Processes used to deepen a trance state, typically after initial induction. Can be used at any time during hypnosis to deepen a trance to a specific stage. To deepen we must create a trigger and then attach going deeper to the trigger.

DEEPER

This word is used frequently in hypnosis it directly links the idea of depth of feeling to depth of trance.

DELTA

Very deep state of hypnosis where brainwave cycles are right down to .5 Hz.

DELUSION

A belief that is unwaveringly held despite evidence to the contrary.

DEPRESSION

Clinical depression is a real mental health condition. Although ego strengthening, confidence and self esteem therapies can be used in hypnosis to help in this dissorder, it should be done in conjunction with qualified health workers.

DESCRIPTIVE

Always use very descriptive language when inducing trance and delivering scripts. Appeal to all the senses make things as real as possible for the subject.

DESENSITISE

Reducing the sensitivity to a particular stimulus.

DIAGNOSIS

The identifying of a disorder

DIRECT SUGGESTION

A therapy type where you simply suggest a change directly to the subject for example. In future will no longer smoke cigarettes.

DISSOCIATION

This is the feeling of being detached from oneself. One example of dissociation is when using the ideomotor response technique, we are encouraging a response from the finger rather than the person themselves. Another example of dissociation is in the language we use. If you study most of my inductions either here or in my other books on close inspection you will notice a detached way of referring to the subject. Such as 'now just let those eyes close' instead of 'Now just let your eyes close'. It is a subtle yet important switch from the word yours to those. This encourages dissociation and can help in most circumstances. Making the experience less personal can be a very powerful aid when dealing with traumatic events during regression coupled with the 'as if' statement it is an essential safeguard.

DOGMA

A firmly held belief. These beliefs are handed down by authority and are held without the need for evidence.

DOUBLE BIND

This is a technique used to give the the appearance of choice when really there is only one. 'Would you like to go into trance now or in a moment?' this is a perfect example as it presupposes that the subject will go in to trance it is not a matter of if just a matter of when.

DOWN

Hypnotic word in itself suggests depth to a subjects subconscious. Used frequently in deepeners for this reason. Staircases, elevators etc all go **down** during deepeners.

DREAM ANALYSIS

The analysing of dreams in search of underlying motives. Or symbolic representations of issues.

DRUG INDUCED HYPNOSIS

Exactly what it says. Using drugs to induce a trance state.

THE E's

EGO

Me, I, the core which all psyco-activity revolves.

ELMAN

Dave Elman lived from 1900 to 1967. Multi talented musician, radio host and hypnotist. Created the highly effective Elman induction which is considered a guaranteed hypnotic induction due to the choices given during the induction.

ELMAN INDUCTION

A very effective rapid hypnosis induction created by Dave Elman. It is considered the best gauranteed induction by many hypnotists since it is completely permissive and relies upon he subject to pace themselves into trance with the help of the hypnotist. Created by Dave Elman the renowned hypnotst, author and radio show host.

Below is the Elman induction word for word. However it was originally used in 1963, that's fifty years ago, it is still generally accepted that it is a basis for a good induction but needs updating due to the wording being outdated but also there is quite a lot of questioning of the subject and this may have a tendency to unravel the trance slightly. Especially if there is any misunderstanding. So first will be the induction in pure form and next my own modified version.

The Elman induction:

Will you just take a good long deep breath and close your eyes...now relax the muscles around your eyes to the point where those eye muscles won't work and when you're sure they won't work....test them and make sure they won't work...test them....get complete relaxation in those muscles around the eyes.......now let that feeling of relaxation go right down to your toes...in a moment were going to do this again and when we do it a second time you're going to be able to relax ten times as much as you're relaxed already....now open your eyes... close you're eyes....completely relax...let yourself be covered with a blanket of relaxation...now the third time we do it you'll be able to double the relaxation which you have...open your eyes...now relax...im going to lift your hand and drop it and if you've followed instructions up to this point that hand will be just as limp as a dishrag and will just plop into your lap...let me lift it...dont you lift it...let it be heavy...thats good...but let's open and close the eyes again and double that relaxation and send it right down to your toes...let that hand be as heavy as lead...you'll feel it when you've got the relaxation...now you've got it...you could feel that couldn't you?.. that's complete physical relaxation...but I want to show you how you can get mental relaxation as well as physical...so I'm going to ask you to start counting...when I tell you to...from a hundred backwards...each time you say a number....double your relaxation...and by the time you get down to ninety eight you'll be so relaxed there won't be any more numbers...start with the idea of making that happen and watch it happen...count out loud please..(100)...double your relaxation and watch the numbers start disappearing...(99)...watch the numbers start disappearing...(98)...now they'll be gone...make it happen...you've got to do it...I can't do it...make them disappear...dispel them...make them vanish.

At this point the subject participation gets quite intense.

Below is a modified Elman induction complete with integrated deepener:

Take a nice deep breath and hold it...

Now let that breath out and close your eyes...

Now take your attention to your eyelids...

You can relax your eyelids so much that they just..

Won't..

Work...

Once you are sure that you have relaxed them completely...

Hold on to that relaxation...

Now check them and make sure they won't work...

Good now stop checking...

And go even deeper relaxed...

Now send that feeling of relaxation down through your entire body from your head to your toes...

Good...now I am going to check that you understood my instructions...

In a moment...

Not yet..

But in a moment im going to lift up your arm and drop it...

Don't help me...

Let your arm be completely limp and loose...

Let me do all the work...

(lift and drop arm about 3 inches)

Good...

As you just go deeper...

Because human beings do better with practise...

We are going to do that again...

And when we do it a second time it will be as if you were ten times more deeply relaxed...

Open your eyes...

Close your eyes and relax...

Test those eyelids again...

To make sure...

Good stop testing and...

Completely relax...

And send that relaxation right the way down throughout the whole body...

Good and when we do this one more time...

It will be as if you go twice as deeply relaxed as you are...

Good and now open your eyes...

Close your eyes...

And go twice as deep twice as relaxed...

And again send that feeling of deep relaxation throughout your body...

Right from the top of your head down to your toes...

Now let us relax your mind...

Really allow your mind to relax...

Just as your body is deeply relaxed...

In a moment...

Not quite yet...

I'm going to count backwards from one hundred...

And as i count down you will notice that...

After each number has gone it's as if your relaxation just doubles...

And You can relax so much that...

After I say the number you can allow it to...

Just disappear...

It doesn't take long...

Just a few numbers before they completely cisappear...

After each number you can just double your relaxation...

And then just let it disappear...

100 now let the number disappear and double your relaxation.....

99 deeper, deeper relaxed and the number just fades

98 and the numbers fade away just fade away...

To nothing, nothing, nothing...

Want that and you can have it...

Very easily...

And when all the numbers are gone ...

You can just allow your right index finger to raise up...

To let me know that all the numbers are gone...

Good...

In a moment I will count to three...

And on the count of three you will open your eyes and look up at me...

And when I click my fingers and say sleep...

Your eyes will close...

And you will go twice as deeply relaxed...

Each time your eyes close you become more relaxed...

Nod your head when you understand.....

Good one...two...three open your eyes and look up at me...

(click) close your eyes and go deeper.....

Good...

One ...two...three open your eyes and look up at me...

And sleep...

As if you meant to go twice as deep again.

Repeat this several times looking for signs of trance deepening also random arm drops deepen the trance dramatically.

EIGHT WORD INDUCTION

Probably the most elegant of all inductions. It is exactly what it says the wording is as follows;

Push on my hand...

Close your eyes...

Sleep!

This is done with a hand drop shock, the subject hand is placed on top of the hypnotists then the above wording is used as the hypnotist pulls his hand away.

EMBEDDED COMMANDS

Commands to an individual hidden within a conversation, can be done as a complete command using body language and speech inflections to give the instruction weight

Also which is very popular in advertising is to place key words within a sentence and again changes in the vocal and or visual tone.

EMBEDDED SUGGESTION

Same as embedded commands above.

EMERGENCE

The act of bringing someone out of trance at the end of a hypnosis session. Also known as the awakening and trance termination.

EMPATHY

Understanding the feeling of others. Putting yourself in anothers shoes.

EMPTY CHAIR

A disaccotiation therapy technique whereby the subject projects their own issues to an imaginary person sitting in an empty chair.

ENCOURAGE

The hypnotist should always be encouraging saying things like 'good and excellent' help the subconscious to make the changes it needs. It is like praising a child in order to get the best out of them.

ENTRANCED

Another term for trance.

ERIKSON

The recognised leading authority on clinical hypnosis of recent times is Milton Erickson. During his lifetime he was considered the master of hypnosis using symbolism, metaphors, his work became known as 'Ericksonian Hypnosis'. It was his work which led to the development of NLP by Bander and Grindler.

ESDAILE

James Esdaille used hypnotism extensively even before the term hypnosis was used. He based his technique on mesmerism He is believed to be the pioneer of surgical hypnosis after his success in India, bringing the post surgery mortality rate down from over fifty percent to under eight percent.

ESDAILE STATE

Considered to be the deepest of all hypnotic states, Hypertrance

EUPHORIA

A feeling of deep well being and elation often accompanied by an optimistic outlook. Most people experience this feeling upon emerging from hypnosis, especially if the hypnotist delivers the 'hypnotic gift' during the emergence routine.

EXPECTATION

One of the best convinces available to the hypnotist, in fact it is said that if you have created enough expectation along with belief trance is inevitable. If a subject is expecting 'something' to happen' they are self convincing. The other side to the expectation coin is always give 'em what they think they already know. Example: if you ask someone what they know about hypnosis and they reply that you need a swinging pocket watch and to be told you are getting very sleepy, you would be well advised to include this as part of your induction. if they believe that this is what is required they may resist any other method you try to use.

EXTRASENSORY PERCEPTION

ESP a paranormal term for sixth sense perceptions

EYE CATALEPSY

Or eye lock. Technically wrongly named. It is in fact the phenomena of eyelids locked closed. Used as a convincer and as part of depth testing.

EYE FLUTTER

One of the common signs of hypnosis.

EYE STRAIN

One of the conditions we create to aid in inducing hypnosis. Especially useful when using some of the progressive relaxation techniques. Eye strain is quite literally the eyes or eyelids aching. When closing of eyes is suggested as part of the induction the subject willingly complies. If the correct timing and wording are used it is also a great convincer.

THE F's

FAITH HEALING

Healing which occurs purely because the subject has faith in the operator.

FALL BACK INDUCTION

A rapid and sometimes instant induction often used on stage for dramatic effect. The subject is given suggestions that they are falling backwards and as they do the hypnotist shouts sleep and breaks their fall to the floor.

FALSE MEMORY

A memory implant which occurs during hypnosis. These false memories can occur for a number of reasons, usually purely accidental. Sometimes the wrong style of questioning is used by the operator and information enters the highly suggestible subconscious, since the subconscious cannot differentiate between reality and fiction the problem can occur. Also there may be an event which occured with the subject and has been repressed and because of a badly handled hypnotic session the facts can become jumbled with fiction and again we have false memory. You can of course implant a false memory intentionally, perhaps as a post hypnotic suggestion for comedy purposes. It is hard to imagine why one would want to do this as a permanent false memory though.

FASCINATION

We use fascination as part of the whole fixation and attention narrowing experience. When a subject is fascinated there is a natural tendency to focus more on whatever is causing the fascination. In fact the next time you see a child fascinated with an object look at their face and body. You will see the same trance signs noticeable in hypnosis.

FEAR

This emotion is often used as part of the stage or street show. Fear, awe, belief and expectation are the trademarks of a stage hypnotist. It may seem strange to think that if a potential subject is frightened that they may be hypnotised, that they would be susceptible, but if they haven't run for the hills already that fear works in the hypnotists favour. The subject has convinced themselves that there will be a change and so when they are told to go into trance they go. I have seen subjects so in fear of the whole experience of being on stage etc that when the time finally came just a look from the hypnotist was all it took for them to go into trance.

FREE ASSOCIATION

A fruedian method of allowing a subject to speak for themselves making their own links and associations etc and self healing. More a psychoanalysis tool.

FIFTEEN

This is how many times a suggestion needs to be repeated to the subconscious mind, especially in direct suggestion, in order for it to be accepted as a new habit. The repetition must be exact. Not to be confused with compounding.

FINGER SIGNALLING

One of the ideomotor responses. The finger of the subject is used to answer questions put by the hypnotist.

FIXATION

The fixing in place of anything. An example in hypnosis terms the fixation of the eyes or gaze upon a single object in order to narrow focus and cause eye strain.

FOCUS

Narrowing of the attention on one particular stimuli.

FORGETTING

Losing the ability to recall a memory or memories. Forgetting is part of the repression process the memory is still there it is just inaccessible or forgotten.

FRACTIONATION

The process of inducing trance, awakening and re-inducing trance in quick succession. This is a very effective deepener

FRAMING

A set of elements defining a situation. It is our perspective of the world around us. Framing and reframing is used to assist subjects with improving lifestyles.

FUGUE STATE

A life assumed following amnesia. The person has no recollection of their previous life. They live in complete ignorance of it assuming fully every aspect of their new life.

THE G's

GENITAL TYPE

One of the so called character types. These individuals develop awareness from the age of about five right up to puberty . the main characteristics of this type is their immaturity. They can be extrovert and very unpredictable.

GLOVE ANAESTHESIA

The inducing of numbness to pain in the hand, once achieved the feeling, or lack of, can be transferred to another part of the body. This method is often used in clinical and dental hypnosis.

GO INSIDE

This is one of the classic routes when using progressive relaxation inductions. The subject is guided to internalise noticing their breathing the sensations they are feeling. An example would be the following which is part of a Progressive Relaxation Induction.

Notice each breath that you take...

Feel your chest rise...

As you breath in...

And fall as you exhale...

And as you notice your breathing...

And feeling more relaxed...

With each exhaled breath...

You can think down...

Inside yourself and focus on your toes...

Allow those toes to become completely relaxed...

Tension free...

More relaxed than they have ever been...

And as you feel that relaxation inside your toes...

Notice the relaxation spreading through your feet...

Feel how the feet just relax as much as the toes...

etc... etc... etc.

GOOD

Another power word for hypnotists used between pauses and during feedback loops to praise the subconscious as we move the session forward. Since the subconscious thinks like a 4 Year old this word is high praise and encourages compliance for the next suggestion.

GO WITH YOU

This expression is used in therapy. The reasons are that no matter what happens internally for the subject during trance they will always hear your voice. It is a good safety measure to employ in all sessions. For instance the hypnotist is regressing a person back to a 'past life' whilst experiencing this something distressing begins to happen. You are able to guide your subject away from this. What would happen if the subject believed they really had gone back in time. How could they hear you? So we always use the my voice will go with you expression.

Also it can be a reinforcement statement that the words used in the therapy session will remain with the subject.

GROUP THERAPY

Therapy attended by many subjects with common issues. This style of therapy is often one of self help and peer mentoring. Less effective with specific issues due to the varying susceptibility of different subjects.

THE H's

HABIT

That which is done automatically or 'habitually'. If we perform a task or ritual enough times consciously eventually the subconscious will take over the task and it becomes a habit, freeing up the conscious to get on with more important things.

A good example is driving a car. When we first start to drive it takes tremendous amounts of conscious effort to perform the complex multitude of tasks. Eventually the subconscious takes over most of them leaving us to do the here and now parts like hazard awareness.

HALLUCINATION

Imagining something is real when it is not. Seeing or hearing something which is in fact not there or even not being able to see something that is there. Once a hypnotist suggestions of hallucination are being accepted and acted upon he can be sure that the deeper levels of trance have been reached

HAND CLASP

One of the more common susceptibility tests.

Subjects are asked to interlock their hands ir front of them. Suggestions are them made that their hands are stuck together. Suggestions that they will simply become as if one solid object like a steel bar or that there is very strong glue between their hands.

HAND PASSES

Passing the hand down in front of the subjects eyes when open creates a non verbal instruction to close their eyes. This is also effective on a subject with eyes closed as part of a deepener because of the shadows created.

HEAD NODDING

Asking a subject to nod their head to confirm they accept a suggestion is one of the most powerful tools available to a hypnotist. 'Nod your head when you understand' it is an agrement with the suggestion therefore it will be carried out! Also see biofeedback

HEAD ROTATION

Used during some inductions especially as part of a deeper immediately after an instant induction.

The hypnotist places his hand on the top of the subjects head and gently rotates the head whilst making the suggestions.

HEAL

A return to a normal state after injury infection or illness. Not really a term used in hypnotherapy

HISTORY

Always take as thorough and accurate history from a subject before entering into any type of therapy. Make every effort to understand the client as well as the issue or issues that they have.

HOW LONG DOES IT TAKE TO HYPNOTISE A SOMEONE.

This depends on the subject and the hypnotist. Some people can go into trance very quickly and others take more time. However if the right conditions are created and the correct convinces used an expert hypnotist will be able to hypnotise almost anyone very quickly.

HUMAN BRIDGE

One of the more extreme stage phenomena. Full body catalepsy is induced while the subject is standing upright. Then the subject is lifted onto their backs by assistants whilst remaining rigid then suspended between the back uprights of two chairs. Supported only by their neck and ankles. Then the hypnotist then climbs up onto the stomach of the subject. This is potentially a very dangerous 'trick' , the amount of physical effort needed to maintain this level of muscle tension for an extended period as well as the potential damage from having to support the weight of the hypnotist could cause permanent damage.

HYPERMNESIA

The phenomena of increasing memory recall under hypnosis. There are those that believe that although there is an appearance of greater recollection due to hypnotic suggestion, that these memories are in fact false memories created by the subconscious specifically to comply with the suggestion itself.

HYPERTRANCE

This is a state of very deep trance or hypnosis the very best therapy work is done during this trance state. Often refered to as somnabulism

HYPNOANALYSIS

Effectively psycho-analysis whilst under hypnosis is very fast and effective. Aligning the subconscious thoughts and activity with the persons beliefs of who they are without the protracted need to have years of therapy. It is said that hypnoanalysis and hypnotherapy are at least ten times quicker at reaching the desired conclusion as psycho-analysis and pcychotherapy. It is actually imeasurable but these seem very corservative estimates. If we the hypnotist can achieve in one sessior that which takes a psycho-analyst years. Well you do the math.

HYPNOBIRTHING

The use of hypnosis and self hypnosis in childbirth reducing stress for mother and child as well as increasing comfort levels. Helping to enhance the experience and control discomfort.

HYPNOLOGY

The study of hypnosis and hypnotic phenomena

HYPNOSIS

The state in which a person becomes more open to suggestion than in the normal waking state. Often referred to as trance due to the physical appearance often observed I.E. the zombie look. Hypnosis is a state somewhere between sleeping and being awake. We are in a mild hypnotic state when we daydream. It is not as some believe a full sleep state, even though REM sometimes occurs.

HYPNOTHERAPY

The combination of hypnosis and therapy. During hypnotherapy the hypnotist makes suggestions directly to the subconscious. Generally accepted to be twelve times quicker than psychotherapy.

HYPNOTIC

Anything deemed to aid in the inducement of the hypnotic state.

HYPNOTIC CONTRACT

In the therapy room this should be a properly written document stating all the procedures and expected outcomes as well as the financial arrangements and any exclusions. This kind of contract should be signed by both parties prior to therapy and after all histories and any other relevant information is gathered. As far as stage and or street go at some stage you should simply get verbal permission preferably in earshot of witnesses. A Simple ' so are you ready and willing to try hypnosis?

HYPNOTIC GIFT

The hypnotic gift should be given to anyone and everyone who is hypnotised. It is the final post hypnotic suggestion. The gift should be with regard to how the person will feel and behave after hypnosis. For example;

When you wake from this trance...

You will feel as if you have had a five hour full body massage...

And an eight hour deep sleep...

You will feel refreshed and ready to face the rest of your day with enthusiasm and confidence...

In fact you will find that from this day forward you have the confidence to achieve anything.

You set your mind to...

Feeling better and better about yourself...

As each day passes...

And with each and every day this confidence...

This knowing...

That you are capable of anything you want...

Will grow and grow.

HYPNOTIC STARE

This is that disconcerting Dracula like glare that some hypnotists are able to use. Although it appears that the hypnotist is staring into the subjects soul through the eyes, it is in fact an optical illusion. The stare is directed at the bridge of the subjects nose. To perfect the hypnotic stare practice is required. Look at the bridge of your own nose in a mirror without blinking. Do this regularly until you can hold the stare for a few minutes. Or at least long enough to make your subject look away. The hypnotic stare is an uncomfortable thing for the person on the receiving end. Another convincer that once the game begins 'something will happen'.

HYPNOTIC VOICE

In terms of therapy the hypnotic voice should be soothing, steady and calming. Since we rely so heavily on relaxation the hypnotists voice should be relaxing. It should resonate from the bottom of your chest a sort of diaphragm driven voice. In all other circumstances the hypnotic voice must reflect the situation. Exciting and loud for stage etc.

HYPNOTIST

A person able to guide another into the state of hypnosis, it is thought by many and I would not necessarily disagree, that all hypnosis is self hypnosis and the hypnotist simply helps to direct a non skilled person into a state of self hypnosis.

HYPOGENIC ZONES

Zones on the body which can help to induce the hypnotic state. They can also be used for silent inductions.

HYPNOGOGIC STATE

Daydreaming state the eyes are wide open but the subject is so focussed as if in ther own world. It is said that daydreaming is a healthy passtime neccessary for our mental well being.

HYPNOIDAL STATE

A state of hypnosis without being hypnotised. We all experience hypnoidal states, they include Daydreaming hypnogogic state (as you fall asleep) hypnopompic state (as you wake up) shock. The effects of this state are similar to regular hypnosis the subject is suggestible however if the hypnoidal state has been brought on by shock it is then often associated with amnesia of the causative incident. Much like a car accident victim being in a dazed state. Not only will he follow instructions given to him he may lose all recolection of the event itself. Part of the built in self preservtion system we all have.

HYSTERIA

Mental illnesses resulting in and from emotional conflict.

THE I'S

IDENTIFYING TRANCE

The first rule of identifying trance is that there are so many subtle signs that you could fill an entire book. There are some very common obvious signs as listed below. More importantly the hypnotist should be looking for change. Any sort of change no matter how small can be an indicator of the hypnotic or trance state being present. If the change is as a direct result of the operators suggestion then you can be almost certain that the trance state exists.

Common signs of trance are:

Waxy ultra relaxation of facial muscles.

A day dream expression.

Dilation of the pupils.

Complete relaxation of the torso.

Feet falling to the sides.

Head falling to the side or forwards

Eye lids fluttering.

Eyes watering.

Driibling or drooling.

Stomach rumbles.

NOTE: Whenever you notice signs of trance feed the information back to the subject see biofeedback loop.

IDEOMOTOR RESPONSES

These are physical responses caused by the subconscious mind caused by external input usually verbal suggestion.

The head nod, finger signalling, pendulum response are all forms of ideomotor responses. A good example of its uses in finger signalling such as:

In a moment I'm going to ask your subconscious mind...

Your honest mind...

The mind that knows all...

About you...

Some questions...

I don't want you to answer me...

I just want you to think of the answer...

The answer will be either yes or no..

If the answer is yes I want you to just keep thinking YES...YES...YES

And as you think the word yes...

You will notice that...

Your right index finger...

That's the finger next to your thumb...

Your pointing finger...

That finger will rise up off of your leg...

Whenever you think the word yes...

Your right finger will rise...

Nod your head when you understand.

This can be tested or move on to the no response. Where the left index finger is designated the 'no' answering finger. You may ask if you can elicit a head nod why not use this as the ideomotor response. It is true that this may be used however it may be regarded by the subject as actually answering the question and elicit non truthful answers. If while in trance it appears that you are asking the finger a question and there is detachment of responsibility on the part of the subject more honest information is passed.

IMAGINATION

The creation of images within the mind. To imagine we use the 'minds eye' or 'minds ear' . the process of imagining can be completely unrealistic it is effectively the opposite of intellectual thought. The more imaginative a subject the more susceptible. In order to perform any task we must first be able to imagine doing it. Also whenever there is a struggle between intellect and imagination the imagination will always win!

A good example of this is after we have seen a horror movie. Intellectually we are more than aware that the ghosts ghouls etc are not in the wardrobe in the dark bedroom in our own house. This does not however stop us from getting spooked walking into the darkened room.

This is one of the most important qualities a subject can possess. The better the imagination the more susceptible they wil be. Before we can acheive anything we must imagine it first. In therapy a good imaginationis invaluable. Before we make a change we must imagine it.

INCONGRUENCE

The disparity between what is being said verbally and what is being projected non verbally. We may say one thing whilst our tone of voice and or our body language and o⁻ expressions are 'saying something else. Someone may tell us they feel fine but their non verbal's are telling us the complete opposite.

INDUCTION

The process of inducing the hypnotic state in a subject, or inducing self hypnosis.

INDUCTION TYPES

Shock

Relaxation

Distraction

Confusion

Visualisation

Non verbal

INHIBIT

To restrict the movement. For instance when creating catalepsy in limbs for depth testing and sketches etc.

INHIBITION

In context of stage work where subjects loose their inhibitions and carry out the most strange suggestions.

INSTANT INDUCTION

Exactly as it sounds, these inductions typically take less than 2 seconds. They rely on shock and awe. The most common instant induction are the pattern interrupt.

INTELLIGENCE

One of the common misnomas of hypnosis is that only the weak and feable minded can be hypnotised. This may have something to do with the popular ideas that hypnosis is mind control. This in fact could not be further from the truth. Hypnosis is a skill which must be learned by the subject. Intelligence is an absolute requirement the better a subject understands an instruction or suggestion the better he or she will be able to comply.

INPUT

The recieving of stimuli into the mind from any of the senses.

THE J's THE K's AND THE L's

JUST

One of our power words. When we use the word just as part of the hypnotic experience we are implying that it will take no effort, that it will be easy, that it will just happen.

You can just allow this wonderful feeling to flow across your entire body.

KINESTHETIC TYPES

A tactile type of person. This type of person will communicate in a very tactile and emotional style. When speaking they will use words like I feel this way or that way, I'm hurting and when describing dealing with an issue they will say things like tackle and grasp. kinesthetic types will look down when accessing memories or having internal dialogue.

LAW DOMINANT EFFECT

The more powerful emotion will tend to overcome and replace weaker. The stronger the emotional content and context of suggestion the better effect it will have. It is why we use vivid language and try to apeal to as many senses as possible. Making the suggestion as meaningful as possible.

LAW OF REPETION

The more we are exposed to an idea the more we accept it. This is how we form habits whether bad or good. It also means that we can change a habit by using repetition. Also referred to as Coues law of repeated concentration. Therefore repeating is the mantra for the hypnotist. It can be very boring saying the same thing over and over again. But it can be very beneficial to the subject. It can reinforce a suggestion but also it is used to drive the message home within the subconscious. We could if we were so inclined change a habit simply by repetition once the subject is hypnotised. With the subject in a highly suggestible state the law of concentrated attention is used very effectively. Notwithstanding the law of dominant effect

LAW OF REVERSED EFFECT.

The more conscious effort we put into achieving a particular goal the more the opposite effect will actually result. As in the more you try to open your eyes the tighter they become stuck tight together.

LEAD

For the hypnotist this refers to part of the building rapport process as well as directing the whole hypnotic process.

When attempting to build rapport after matching the subject we would attempt to lead them. This is also known as pacing. When we ask someone to take deep breaths during induction for instance, we take deep breaths ourselves encouraging the subject to copy or match us. This type of pacing is actually quite overt but when pressed for time it is a perfect start to having rapport with the subject.

The other way in which we lead is when we take the subjects through the hypnotic process. Some would say that all hypnosis is self hypnosis and that the hypnotist himself is just a guide or leader of sorts.

A word of caution with regard to leading. Whenever asking questions during regression keep them as open as possible. Inadvertent leading can be the cause of false memories for the subject.

LEADER

In any sort of session therapeutic or entertainment the hypnotist is the leader and must remain so in order to guide the subject the hypnotist must be in control of the session, this does not mean to say he is in control of the subject. See mind control

LEFT BRAIN

Not really a correct term, left hemisphere of the brain is what is meant. This is the side of the brain which deals with logic.

LETHARGY

Slow response or movement. This is one of the classic signs of deeper states of hypnosis. It appears to be a sort of unwillingness to perform tasks suggested to them. In fact it is just a very common hypnotic phenomenon.

LEVITATING ARM.

One of the more common suggestibility tests/ convincers. The subject is told that their arm will rise of their lap. Eyes can be open or closed.

LIGHTENING

The opposite of deepening, it may be desirable under cirtain circumstances to bring a subject up into a lighter trance.

LIMBIC SYSTEM

Part of the brain responsible for our unconscious behaviour its actions are completely uncensored and automatic. I'ts the unconscious reaction to stimuli. Our non verbal behaviour is controlled by the limbic sysrem. It does not use logic or imagination like the conscious or sub conscious, rather it reacts to the animal instinct of pain or pleasure.

LOGIC?

The thinking mind this is the mind that calculates, reasons and rationalises. When we refer to logic we are referring to the function of the conscious mind. Logic resides in the left hemisphere of the brain.

LOOK DOWN.

denotes a kinesthetic type

LOOK SIDEWAYS

Denotes an auditory type

LOOK UP

Denotes a visual type

Also used as suggestion, in order to cause eyestrain helping with subsequent induction.

LUNAR CYCLE

It is said that to make a permanent change to a habit takes one lunar cycle. About twenty eight days.

LOOSING NUMBERS

Very effective deepener used in the Elman induction and several others. Can be used in its own right

THE M's

MAGNETISM

In the early days of hypnosis Franz Anton Mesmer believed that there existed a magnetic force within all humans. He would use magnets to heal placed about a patients body in order. He discarded the magnets and made use of what he described as his own 'animal magnetism' this animal magnetism is believed to be a form of hypnotism and is why the trance state is often referred to as being mesmerised.

MEDITATION

A form of self induced trance. Used by many for enlightenment or self improvement. It could be said that being in a state of hypnosis is the same experience as being in a meditative state.

MEDIUM

One of the hypnotic levels or stages.

Also a person that claims to be able to speak to departed souls. I'm not really a believer in the gift of medium-ship however I do have an open mind when it comes to anything that cannot be readily explained, you never know! What I do know is that there are many people gifted in the art of cold reading.

MEMORY

The mental process of storing information from the past, events ideas etc.

MEMORIES

Recollections past events. Every single experience sight sound touch etc is held in our subconscious as a memory. Most of which we do not or cannot access under normal circumstances. Some of these memories can even be repressed or suppressed in order to protect us. Under hypnosis it is possible to access all and any of these memories.

MENTAL ILLNESS

Subjects with genuinely professionally diagnosed mental illness should not be hypnotised except where the treatment is part of treatment supervised by a qualified health worker.

MENTALISM

The combination of non verbal reading, hypnosis and deception is used primarily for stage, because of this combination the 'new' term of mentalism has been coined. It relies on various manipulations of the mind not just hypnosis.

MESMER

Friedrich Anton Mesmer was the discoverer of hypnosis. In the late 18th century. His name for the phenomena he discovered was animal magnetism. He was able to cure pople without the need for surgery or medicines. He claimed that all living things had a magnetic fluid flowing around them and that he was able to manipulate this fluid.

MESMERISM

Often people will refer to a person being mesmerised when displaying classic signs of trance. Its a historical by product of the fact that the earliest 'operator' of bygone hypnosis is a man called Mesmer. His terminology for the phenomenon he discovered was magnetism and animal magnetism which also created a sort of by product. If you've ever seen an old Dracula movie where the villain of the piece stars into his victims eyes and they are instantly in a trance and drawn to him, you will know that you are seeing the interpretation of animal magnetism and being mesmerised.

METAPHOR

The use of speech to deliver an idea to the subject. However instead of being direct we use similarities in order to get the message across. So we might tell our subject a story which has nothing to do with them at all. However their subconscious mind will draw similarities between the story and their own circumstances. The message is received and understood and the positive change made. Their was no mention of the actual problem therefore no danger of abreaction or defiance.

MIND

The intangible. When we refer to the mind we are referring to what we consider to be 'me'. The best similarity I can draw is that of an electrical appliance and electricity itself. If you imagine the brain is the same as a toaster. It exists it is tangible it is physical we can quantify it. And the mind as the electricity that run s the toaster. It is intangible you cannot see it but you know it is there.

MIND READING

No one can actually read the mind of another however using various techniques such as waking hypnotism and cold reading, for example, the appearance of mind reading can be given.

MIRROR MATCH LEAD

The basic elements required to build rapport.

MISCONCEPTIONS

Here are a list of misconceptions surrounding hypnosis. Some of these misconceptions may cause resistance in potential subjects therefore it is essential to dispel any and all myths;

Hypnotist have special powers

Only special people are hypnotisable

Only the weak minded can be hypnotised

You are helpless when hypnotised

Hypnosis is sleep

Hypnosis is dangerous to your health

Hypnosis is dangerous to your mind

You can be stuck in hypnosis forever.

Hypnosis is like a drug and you can be addicted

You will instantly remember your whole life

Hypnosis is unnatural

You lose control

You can be made to do anything

MONOIDEISM

The name that Baird tried to give to hypnotism after he learned that although similar, hypnosis is not sleep.

MONOTONY

Used in old style inductions usually as part of progressive relaxation and eye strain. As the word suggests it is a sort of boredom technique. The voice is devoid of emotion with no change whatsoever. Thankfully just about a thing of the past. However when learning hypnosis from scratch it is a good starting point. Also be aware of some subjects expectation. I would say always go with what they think they know.

MULTIPLE PERSONALITY

A person with multiple personality disorder has more than one personality. Or rather one or more sub personalities. They are very susceptible to hypnosis. Not to be confused with schizophrenia.

MUSCLES

Relaxing and tensioning of muscles is used as indicators of trance. For depth testing and of course convincing.

MUTUAL HYPNOSIS

A system whereby two people hypnotise each other for mutual benifit. A form of mutual hypnosis can occur inadvertantly when the hypnotist himself may be susceptible and become hypnotised whilst attempting to induce trance in others

MY VOICE WILL GO WITH YOU

This is a very useful statement to use as a safeguard. It ensures that no matter what the circumstances the subject will hear what you have to say. Say you were performing past life regression therapy, the subject regresses and believes they speak a foreign tongue, they might not respond to the hypnotist unless you use this statement. Also should the subject experience an abreaction the hypnotist must be confident that their suggestions are heard.

THE N'S

NEGATIVE

Avoid anything negative within hypnosis. Everything about the experience for the subjct should be positive especially the final outcome. Also we must understand the subconscious mind does not understand negative language. If you use negative language you are performing a sort of reversed effect of whatever therapy you are attempting. It can become like an upside down embedded suggestion or command. 'you will not smoke more cigarettes after today's session' since the subconscious will ignore completely the word 'NOT' this is what will actually be heard 'you will smoke more after today's session'. So you see it imperative that you never use negative language.

NEGATIVE HALLUCINATION

Not being able to see something which is there. When suggestions that the subject cannot see something that is actually there are accepted then it can be assumed that a very deep level of trance has been achieved and that any suggestion given thereafter will be accepted. A good example of this is when the stage hypnotist suggests that the subject/s are unable to see him, the hypnotist' then he walks around the stage carrying various items. The subjects actually see floating objects.

NEGATIVE SUGGESTION

The only time the hypnotist should use negative suggestion is when deliberately employing the law of reversed effect such as when using the 'try and you cannot' statement.

NERVOUSNESS

For the purpose of stage this can be a handy thing along with awe, fear, expectation etc. A little nervousness can be a great asset when inducing shock inductions. However in the therapy room nervousness is not a good thing, remember that the subject is in therapy in order to make a positive change. This implies that whatever the issue it is perceived by the client as a negative thing in their life. Often this can be very embarrassing for them. So we should do all we can to eradicate nervousness. We do this by using correct tone of voice, mirroring, pacing building rapport to the point that trust exists and the nervousness is gone. Sometimes the nervousness can be quite evident but at other times it can be not so obvious. In order to look for the signs you will need to be a good reader of body language.

Signs of nervousness

Fidgeting

Lack of eye contact

Shrinking

Forgetting

MuddlingExcessive chattering

Lip biting

Hair pulling

Finger tapping

Needing the toilet

Self hugging (comforting)

Self stroking (comforting)

NON VERBAL COMUNICATION

Often referring to body language. This implies that the positioning of the body is what body language is all about. This is true to a point. Non verbal is everything that a person is telling you except the actual words coming out of their mouths. Non verbal communication also includes facial expression, tone of voice, micro expressions and eye accessing.

NON VERBAL INDUCTION

Inducing the hypnotic state without saying anything except initial instruction. Verbal deepeners are still used once the trance is achieved. The induction relies on expectation and belief completely. Convincers are internalised and are therefore very powerfull. These inductions vary from simply leading the subject with simple half eye closures performed by the hypnotist until the subject closes their eyes right up to the waving of arms and such.

NORMAL NEUROTIC PSYCOTIC

Someone once said to me 'the three steps to madness'.

1. A normal reaction is one that is commonly accepted as being reasonable to the stimulus. So a normal person might see a spider and remove it from the house or not go near it.

2. A neurotic reaction would be to put your feet up on a chair and refuse to go near the spider and insist on someone removing it for you

3. A psycotic reaction would be to refuse to go out of the house in case there might be spiders there without there being any prior knowledge.

In simple terms:

Neurosis is an exaggeration of normal behavior

Psychosis is an exaggeration of neurosis.

Hence the three steps to madness analogy.

NOTICE

A hypnotic word used in feedback loops. Drawing the attention to notice changes in order to create further change.

NUERO LINGUISTIC PROGRAMMING

NLP the technique of using language patterns to bring about change in behaviour. It is akin to embedded suggestion given in a waking state. The use of NLP language patterns under hypnosis is almost a given when you see that it is so close to the embedded command route.

NEUROTIC

A person who displays abnormal behaviours. This person understands and accepts the behaviour is not normal and would like to change that behaviour. Usually not accepted as a genuine mental illness.

THE O's

O.C.D.

Obsessive Compulsive Disorder. Obsessive behaviours and thoughts used in order to stave of anxiety. It could be said that phobias are a form of O.C.D. These disorders can be dealt with using hypnosis as part of treatment in conjunction with mental health professionals.

OPEN QUESTION

A question asked with no presupposed answers in mind. Whenever we are truth seeking such as in therapy or regression we should use open questions. The opposite of a open question is a closed question and the ultimate closed questions are covered in double binds. Imagine you have a subject deeply hypnotised and regressed to a point in childhood and you want to know if there are any people in the room and if yes who. You phrase the question in a closed manner 'who is in the room with you? ' there is very little wiggle room for the subconscious. It may say to itself 'ah there are people here I've just been told so, all I must do is picture who they are'. If you ask the question in an open format the answer can be more 'honest'. 'Describe to me what you can see as you look around the room'. Now the subconscious will look around the memory and describe what it sees, if there are people there he will tell you not the other way around. Listen to a past life regression recording and see how many closed and open questions there are.

OPERATOR

Another term for hypnotist.

ORAL TYPE

One of the so called character types. They develop awareness up to the age of around three. They can be introvert and reserved.

They are very self-conscious types. They can be very much all or nothing displaying similar characteristics of bi polar disorder.

ORIGINAL CAUSE

Everything must start somewhere. The symptom or effect is created as a response to a repressed or suppressed event. The event is called the original cause once this is discovered and dealt with the symptom will dissapear.

OVERLOAD

Used as part of the confusion induction. Overloading the consscious mind in order to confuse the critical factor and allow access to the subconscious.

THE P'S and Q

PACING

The NLP term for leading during rapport building. Fist we mirror and match then we pace the subject. Using subtle body language movements and also language patterns. To pace is to lead your subject to a more appropriate behaviour pattern

PANICK ATTACK

A short period of intense fear with similar symptoms to anxiety attack often associated with phobias.

PAST LIFE

What it says on the tin really, a life previously lived. To accept the idea of a past life or lives we must accept the existence of reincarnation.

PAST LIFE REGRESSION

The technique of using regression therapy to regress back further than the subjects birth. There are many believers in reincarnation and past life regression hypnosis is big business. I like to keep an open mind on such subjects. From a pureley cynical point of view knowing that false memory syndrome may occur at any time my advise would be to always record all aspects of a past life regression session. Listen or watch any such recordings with absolute impartiality, look out for leading and misleading statements by both hypnotist and subject. Keep an open mind before you decide on the validity of whatever may have occurred.

PARAMNESIA

The phenomena of having a false memory. A recollection of something that did not happen. see false memory syndrome

PARTS THERAPY

The dividing up of the individuals psyche. Making the various parts responsible for different actions then bringing the parts together in harmony by reframing.

PATTERN INTERRUPT

This is the term for a group of inductions. There are certain things that we do so regularly that we do them without thinking, things like shaking hands or even sitting down. If these patterns are interrupted midstream so to speak our critical factor goes into a sort of limbo mode for just a half a second or so. During this time if it is offered comfort from this unusual interruption it will accept it. It is seen in the classic handshake induction used by most stage hypnotists as a means of impressing the audience. Even though during these inductions shock is an element do not confuse them with a pure shock induction.

PAUSE

Very important during suggestions. It is important to allow the subconscious time to absorb the suggestion fully. Pauses should be used strategically during therapy to add weight. Also during trance induction. Look at inductions elsewhere in this book and in my others and you will see the parenthesis used to imply pauses

PENDULUM TEST (CHEVREUL'S PENDULUM)

As is suggested a pendulum can be used to test suggestibility of a subject. Some very elaborate versions of the test have been devised but it only needs to very simple and can be used as a vehicle to seamless induction as with most suggestibility test.

The subject holds a piece of string between forefinger and thumb. At the other end of the peice of string, which only needs to be about a foot (30 cm's) long, a weight is attached to ensure it hangs.

Suggestions are given with regard to the weight swinging in various directions until the pendulum does indeed move. This is

80

caused by micro movements in the hand caused by the subconscious acceptance of the suggestions. A great test/ convincer/ induction start.

Another use of the pendulum can be for non verbal communication with the subconscious. By having the pendulum swing in a certain way in response to questioning a conversation can take place between therapist and subject either in trance or not.

PERSUASION

The art or encouraging another person to accept a change.

PERCEPTION

The individuals view of the world around them. Perception is in deed the individuals reality it colours their view of everything. Therefore the saying that perception is everything is very true.

PERMISSIVE

A style of hypnosis used with certain character types, it allows the subject to remain in control.

PHOBIA

Phobia is simply a symptom of a repressed event. A fear of the unknown. Except that the fear of the originating event has attached itself symbolically to something in the here and now. The symbolism changes from subject to subject but the process remains the same.

Originating event

Repression

Symptom

PHYSICAL SYMPTOMS

Physical anxiety symptoms can arise, sometimes manifesting as ulcers and rashes instead of phobias.

PHYSIOLOGICAL

In hypnosis it is possible to cause physiological changes in the body simply by using the imagination. Burn marks can be produced by suggesting that the subject has been burned. Once something is imagined it can be, coupled with the fact that the subconscious cannot differentiate between real and imagined and it is easy to see how this is possible. This is in fact the basis of psychosomatic disorders.

PHYSYCHOANALYSIS

The analysing of a person psychiatric well being for the purpose of therapy. Widely accepted that it takes about twelve time longer to get the same results through phsycotherapy than it does through hypnotherapy.

POSITIVE

Everything done with regard to hypnotherapy should be done in a positive manner. All references should show hypnosis in a positive light, right down to suggestions given everything must be positive. This is the only way that a positive outcome can be reached no matter the purpose of using hypnosis.

POSITIVE HALLUCINATIONS

This is the phenomena of imagining the existence of something when in reality it is not there, in the entertainment setting it is used to great effect. Having your subjects imagine they are under attack by a swarm of flies is always a crowd pleaser. In therapy it is more likely to be used as part of depth testing. Once a subject is hallucinating we can be sure they are deeply hypnotised.

POST HYPNOTIC AMNESIA

Amnesia which occurs after the trance state has ended. This can occur naturally and can be induced by suggestion. The most common and effective amnesia script used by hypnotists is;

You can forget to remember and remember to forget.

POST HYPNOTIC SUGGESTION

A suggestion given whilst the subject is hypnotised with the express purpose that it be carried out after the subject is awake. These come in two distinct categories. There is the type that is carried out during a performance lets say. So the subject is told eyes open wide awake and then they carry out the suggestion. Although this appears to be a post hypnotic suggestion in reality the subject is still in trance they have not been fully awakened they just have their eyes open. Then there is the genuine post hypnotic. The suggestion is given that at some time it the future the subject will carry out a certain task then they are fully awakened. Then the task is carried out.

POSTURAL SWAY

Used primarily as a suggestibility test. It is a good convincer too and when used as a a final test can lead straight into a shock falling induction. The postural sway test goes like this; stand behind the subject tell them to stand up straight with their feet together, tap their feet together gently using your foot, this encourages compliance, then continue verbally with.

I want you to imagine that there is a rigid iron bar in your shoulders...

Right across your back...

An iron bar connecting your shoulder blades...

Now imagine that my hands are powerful magnets...

The most powerful magnets in the world...

And as I put my hands up behind you...

You can feel those magnets...

Pulling on the iron bar...

Gently at first...

And getting stronger and stronger...

I won't let you fall...

Feel yourself falling falling falling...

Falling back towards those magnets.

This is the traditional or long version. If after performing previous tests you believe you have a highly susceptible subject or you have created a high level of expectancy and belief you can move

on to the beautifully simple and infinatley more impressive short version as follows.

Stand behind the client again tap the feet into position and say this:

I don't know exactly what will happen...

But don't worry I will not let you fall back...

Whatever happens I will catch you.

That's it. If you want to go to the next level you can do this non verbally. Do the foot tap. Then move in front of the subject. Stand about three feet in front of them hold your hands out in front of you at waist height about three feet apart. Look at the subject using the hypnotic stare. Smile and start to slowly lean back, really slowly, this movement must be imperceptible to the human eye. Your movement backwards should be no more than a millimetre a second. The subject will fall forward because of the non verbal signals.

Now to the real power stuff. You caught them by the shoulders. Now stand them up straight saying nothing, give a few very slight shakes to let them know you are making them stand up. Then simply go around and stand behind them. Take a few deep audible breaths. Presto they will fall back into your arms!

POWER WORDS

These are words which carry weight when used wisely they will improve not only your ability to induce trance and perform very effective deepeners but also get the very best results for your subjects when it comes to making those positive changes.

On the next page is a list of some of the most useful and frequently used power words available to the hypnotherapist.

Breathe

Calm

Comfortable

Decreasing

Deep

Deeper

Down

Drift

Drifting

Feel

Focus

Gently

Good

Increasing

Just

Notice

Now

Peaceful

Pleasant

Quietly

Realise

Relax

Remember

Sleep

Slow

Softly

Those

When

When

Whilst

POWER PHRASES

All tension melts away

All the way

Allow yourself

And as you

Every muscle fibre and tissue in your body

Focus your attention

Good

In a moment not quite yet

In a way that makes sense to you

In your own time

Notice noticing

Pay attention to

Really feel that feeling

That's it

That's right

The deeper you go the better you feel the better you feel the deeper you go

The more you x the more y

Well done

When I say

PRECONDITION

Everything that happens to the subject prior to the hypnotic induction will affect their beleifs regarding hypnosis. Preconditioning or convincing should be done at every oprtunity. Create the correct very high level of expectancy and belief.

PRE TALK

Any conversation with the subject prior to hypnosis should be considered part and parcel of a pre-talk. We use a pre-talk to achieve several goals. To create the correct mindset for the subject. To dispel misconceptions. To answer any questions and allay any fears. To create expectancy and be.ief in the subject. To start convincing!

PRENATAL EXPERIENCE

Regressing a subject back beyond birth and into the womb. A good reason for using the term my voice will go wizh you. It implies they will understand what is being said no matter the conditions.

PROFESSIONALISM

The hypnotist should be professional at all times. This means that you should use your skills in a respectfully manner employing your best judgement and respect at all times.

PROGRESSION

This is the opposite of regression. The subject is taken forward in time. Used in timeline therapy in order for the subject to visualise all the benefits of the positive change they have made.

PROGRESSIVE RELAXATION INDUCTION (PRI)

This is your traditional induction focus the attention and relax the mind and body gradually until trance is achieved. I often refer to this as the boredom technique although this is perhaps a little harsh. With so many quick and effective inductions available to the hypnotist it is hard to see why PRI is used. It may have something to do with the perception of giving value for money. Although I much prefer rapid induction coupled with deepeners.

PSYCHONEUROIMMUNOLOGY

It is recently been postulated emotional events influence the subjects immunity to illness and the in turn the immune system influences the brains interpretation of emotional events, the classic vicious circle (in the negative sense). In the positive conotation. We think we will get well we get better and we ultimately get well. This is only recently been clinically accepted.

The basis of hypnotherapy is that the mind affects the body and the body affects the mind.

PSYCHOSIS

A mental health illness where symptoms are so severe they prohibit the subject from functioning normally in everyday life... See NORMAL, NEUROTC, PSYCHOTIC.

PSYCOSOMATIC

Many think that this refers to illness being all in the mind. Not only is it derogatory it is quite wrong. It literally means psyche (the mind) and soma (the body). 'An action of the mind on the body'. It refers to a disorder which involves both mind and body.

So in reality the mind can affect the well being of the body and vice versa.

So we have a repressed unknown memory of an event. A similar event occurs and triggers a physical response so you see apart from biological disorders and injuries most issues that subjects have are psycosomatic.

PSYCOTIC

A person who believes that their abnormal behavior to be normal

QUESTION

For the hypnotist using questions is the groundwork of understanding the subjects or potential subjects. This will lead to the best hypnotic experience for both the subject and the hypnotist.

QUESTIONING TECNIQUE

Whenever questioning a potential subject it is usually better to use open questioning techniques. This is to say that you ask the question in such a way as to illicit an answer in their own words. Avoid closed questions which only require a yes or no response. There is of course exceptions to this rule such as when using questions to create double binds.

THE R's

RAPID INDUCTION

It really is what it says. A hypnotic induction that is induced in just a few seconds. A good example of a rapid induction is the rapid handshake induction. A classic pattern interrupt in which the hypnotist offers his hand for a handshake, as the subject brings his hand up to comply with this social nicety the hypnotist grabs hold of the subjects wrist, brings the hand up in front of the subjects face about three inches away and says...

Look at your hand...

Notice everything...

Especially notice the different shades of colour...

And as you notice noticing that...

You can turn your attention to all the lines...

In your hand...

And in particular....that line...

See all the details of that line...

And as your hand comes down...

Accompany this with pulling the arm gently down

You feel your eyes begin to close...

And feel yourself just relaxing...

Down...down...down...

All the way deep down.

This is a rapid version of the handshake, not to be confused with the shock version of the handshake induction or arm pull.

RAPPORT

The existence of a invisible bond between two or more people. Building rapport can be a complex thing to achieve. Think about personal relationships. Strong friendships romantic relationships within these there exists rapport to varying degrees, regardless how strong it is from one set of individuals to the next, it does exists. It exists out of having shared interests, hobbies, friends, work in fact all manner of things. The basis of rapport is that someone else is like me. And at the subconscious level we all like ourselves. The more like us someone is the more rapport will exist between us.

Building rapport with the aforementioned friends and loved ones happens over a long period. How are we expected to build rapport in a short space of time with someone who is a relative stranger and who, after our session, we may never see again.

We use speech and body language. As a basis if we genuinely care about our work and helping the individual in front of you and they can see this through the congruence between what you say and your body language. This will go a long way to establishing rapport. You can also use contrived techniques such as mirror, matching and pacing. First mirror or match how the subject speaks. Do they communicate kinetically, visually or auditory? Use the same language. If they talk about how they see things they are visual types. If they say things like I hear what your saying they are auditory if they say I feel as if then they are kinetic types. Also match their movements not exactly but when they move say cross their legs or pick up a drink do the same or similar sort of action within a few seconds. Once you've done these things for a while start to lead, pick your drink up or uncross your legs and they will follow. Once you've achieved these things you are now two peas in a pod and the good work can begin. One of the most powerful matching sequences is your breathing.

REFRAMING

Changing ones perception of the world around us and providing alternative, behaviors, patterns

REGRESSION

Literally means going backwards in time to earlier point in the subjects life.

REINFORCE

In hypnotic terms this means to back up the therapy or suggestions in order for it to become permanent. We do this with repetition and compounding statements during therapy. Also we can produce recordings of scripts etc for use outside the therapy room.

REINFORCEMENT TAPES

These are tapes of sessions for use at home by the subject. They can be universal or individually created. They reinforce any therapy that has taken place in the therapists office.

RELAX

The process of reducing tension. A hypnotic power word. One of the ways in which we induce hypnosis.

RELAXATION

The fundamental basis of hypnosis. Even if shock or confusion are used to induce trance relaxation is used to maintain and deepen.

REM

Rapid eye movement. A good indicator that the subject is either experiencing trance or has fallen asleep and is dreaming.

REPLACE

Whenever we remove something from the subconscious we must replace it with something else. The original memory cannot be changed however we can replace the reaction to it. If we do not replace a symptom the subconscious will find its own replacement from its catalogue.

REPRESSION

Not to be confused with suppression repressions are when a memory or event from the past was so painful that it was pushed deep into the subconscious and involuntarily locked away. A person repressing an event will have no conscious knowledge of the original event whatsoever. Repressed memories cause symptoms, releasing the repression through therapy and acceptance removes the symptom

REVIVICATION

This is when a subject has been regressed and then allowed to 'relive' the experience. The subject feels that they are actually re-experiencing whatever happened at that time in their life. This can be a very dangerous road to take when performing regression in order to discover the beginnings of say a phobia. If the phobia was caused by a traumatic event the subject will literally be reliving the event. Better to use the very effective as if statements as safeguard. This way the subject can be an observer detached from the emotional content by means of dissociation. Revivication can easily lead to abreaction.

RIGHT BRAIN

Or rather the right hemisphere of the brain is the part that deals with imagination, emotion and imagery etc.

ROSENTHAL EFFECT

This is a phenomena whereby the therapists own beliefs and preconceptions can impact upon the outcome of therapy. An example may be that a person comes to a therapist to investigate whether past life regression is a possibility, the therapist already believes in this phenomena and his beliefs bias the results, perhaps through inadvertent closed questioning.

THE S'S

SAFE PLACE

Creating a safe place is essential when using regression of any kind for any reason. It is simple to create this safe place, usually it is a case of nominating the chair they are sitting in. Following induction and deepeners and before any work begins tell them that they can return to this chair at anytime. This chair is their safe place and that when you tell them to return to your safe place now, they will feel themselves safe and secure sitting in the chair. Also inform them that no matter what your voice will go with them.

SCRIPT

Pre written inductions or therapy interventions which are read during a session. The up side of using scripts, especially for the beginner, is that the need to remember what to say is negated. The downside is that it is harder to personalise sessions unless the therapist books at least two. One session to take a history and two to deliver the therapy after having written a script. Fortunately the more practice you get the better you will become at using language and inflections and the need for scripts will eventually disappear. Using induction scripts on stage or on the street is virtually impossible, in this case you will have to learn your inductions and deepeners off by heart.

SECRETS

Despite what is said by those not in the know. A hypnotised person cannot be made to give away secrets. In fact a hypnotised person cannot be made to do anything that is against there character or is contrary to their core beliefs.

SELF ESTEEM

This is one of the universals. Whenever you hypnotise someone for whatever reason make sure you add self confidence and self esteem boost to the hypnotic gift.

SELF HYPNOSIS

The ability for an individual to enter trance by themselves. Some use recordings to achieve this others are able to induce self hypnosis unaided. There is a school of thought which is mentioned briefly elsewhere in this book and in some detail in my other books, that all hypnosis is a form of self hypnosis and that the hypnotist is there simply to guide the subject.

SENSORY DEPRIVATION

The removal of all sensory input. Used in brain washing techniques. Subjects will become very highly suggestible without any reference to the outside world.

SESSION

The name we give to the allotted time agreed for the hypnotist to interact with the subject.

SHOCK

One of the methods used to induce instant hypnosis in a subject. I have referred to the handshake induction elsewhere in this book with regard to rapid induction. in the rapid induction the pattern interrupt is used initially which is instantly followed distraction style induction all under a minute. In the shock instant induction we are literally taking one second. So we move in for the handshake and so does the subject. Instead of following through with the handshake we take the wrist of the offered hand with our left hand and move the hand up to the forehead very quickly whilst simultaneously saying SLEEP!

Although this is a very common shock induction it is not my favourite. My preferred instant induction is the hand drop eight word induction.

SHOCK AND AWE

Used to induce instant inductions usually on stage. Probably not appropriate in the therapy room.

SKETCH

Any comedy routine that is performed by the participants in a stage show. The hypnotist suggested to the subjects that they will do something with comedy value either upon opening their eyes or when another trigger is used. This is the whole purpose of the stage performance.

SLEEP

We use this word a lot in the hypnotic world. When we refer to sleep we of course do not mean actual sleep but rather trance. Because of preconception it seems that all subjects are preconditioned to go into trance at the suggestion of sleep by the hypnotist. During therapy it might be wise just to mention to the subject that when you say sleep you do not mean actual sleep. Tell them that you mean them to become deeply relaxed similar to sleep. You don't want your subjects coming to you and actually going to sleep.

SLEEP LEARNING

Recordings played to subjects while they are in genuine sleep. Those asleep are thought to be able to absorb the information better due to the suggestibility of the alpha state.

SOMNAMBULISM

The deepest of all trance like states. I prefer to call this the hyper-trance state. At this level of hypnosis anything is possible. Even the human bridge.

STAGE HYPNOSIS

Hypnosis performed for the purpose of entertainment. Usually in a theatre setting or similar.

START

Everything has a start. Especially referring to repressions.

STAGES OF HYPNOTISM

This refers to depth of hypnotism.

STIGMATA

The appearance of wounds and scars on a subjects body, where there is no physical evidence of wounding. The subconscious simply creates these wounds. Usually atributed to religious events. A very devout christian for instance may show signs of wounds on the wrists and ankles simulating the crusifixion of Jesus Christ this is probably the most widely known example of stigmata.

STREET

Hypnosis performed for entertainment purposes. This is done essentially in bars on the street anywhere that is not an official venue. Using street hypnosis brings certain challenges and the operator must be extra vigilant. Keeping a very close eye on those he has hypnotised and ensuring absolutely that all suggestions are eradicated at the end of any demonstration.

SUBCONSCIOUS

That part of the mind which operates outside conscious control. Sub conscious as the word sub suggests is the part of the mind which operates in the background. It is responsible for storing our memories ideas, beliefs and emotions. It is the store cupboard of the mind. Regardless of how much free will and will power we think we have our life is lived through our subconscious. Our subconscious is resistant to change it likes its comfort zones even when the activity in the comfort zone is a bad thing, like a smoking habit. So because the subconscious stores absolutely every experience you and your five senses have ever had it stores the bad along with the good. Also it thinks like a four year old it doesn't discriminate against reality and fiction. Whatever exists in the subconscious just is. Because it holds our imagination when there is a battle of wills between the conscious and subconscious the subconscious will always win. It can be said then that emotion and imagination will always come out on top of logic.

SUBLIMINAL

These are anything which is deliberately, or not, delivered below conscious awareness to the subconscious. Subliminal messaging is designed to influence people in a very strong emotional way. Subliminal messaging is used in Neurolinguistic Programming as well as in many forms of advertising.

SUGGESTION

A statement made to a person in the hope of influencing them in one way or another. In hypnosis suggestion is every word we utter. Once hypnotised a subject is in a heightened state of suggestibility. Once hypnotised a person is more likely to carry out any suggestion more readily than in a waking state.

SUGGESTABILITY

This is what we refer to with regard to how readily someone may comply with a given suggestion. Some people are naturally more suggestible than others. When in hypnotic trance suggestibility is heightened beyond the norm.

SUGGESTIBILITY/ SUSCEPTIBILITY TESTS

Tests used to determine the suggestibility of a subject and their potential susceptibility to hypnosis potential subjects may or may not be, the rule of thumb is the quicker and more strongly they complete each test the easier they will be to hypnotise. Also they help convince the subject of their own abilities to enter trance. In the therapy room it is better to term them suggestibility exercises since if it is a test and they should feel that they have failed it can be counterproductive. I have also heard them called concentration tests on stage. This is a subtle twist, since we need total concentration from the subject and we need to find our most likely candidates quickly, this challenges the volunteers to do their best, so not only do we see the most susceptible we also guaranteeing that the most cooperative subjects will bekept on stage to work with.

SUPPRESSION

When a memory of a painful or traumatic event is consciously avoided. It is the counterpart to repression. In these cases the subject is fully aware of the initial incident but chooses to 'forget' it.

SYMBOLISM

A technique employed in symptom treatment whereby reference is made to the issue indirectly using symbols. Symbols are very powerful they affect us at the unconscious level.

SYMPTOM

This is a negative reactionary display such as a phobia, anxiety, headaches, warts, stammering, allergies, skin complaints as well as things like obsessions, opinions well just about anything unhealthy. These displays are called symptoms because they are a direct result of a repressed event. So we have a traumatic event in our life it is repressed as part of the defence mechanism and whenever we are confronted with a similar event to the original one we display a symptom.

SYMPOM INTENSIFICATION

Taking the symptom and deliberately intensifying the effect. The subject comes to realise that they can control the symptom.

Effective when a subject has been affected by the law of reversed effect. I.E. the harder they try to rid themselves of the symptom the harder it becomes. When they know they can intensify it at will, then it follows that they can diminish it.

SYMPTOM SUBSTITUTION

Because symptoms are actually extensions of the original event if we remove a symptom as we would in direct suggestion therapy a new symptom will replace the old one.

SYMPTOM SUPRESSION (PHYSICAL SYMPTOMS

In undesirable treatment method, suppression of a symptom will lead to symptom substitution, often the new symptom is worse than the original.

SYSTEMATIC DESENSITISATION

Exposure to a fear in increasing intensity over a period of time gradually dessensitisies the subject to the initial fear and anxiety decreases. This is a psychotherapy technique rarely used in hypnotherapy. I have included this to show that using systematic desensitisation may take several sessions, so etimes years, to eventually 'cure' a patient. The intelligent use of hypnoanalysis and therapy in causative event identification and symptom replacement takes considerably less time.

THE T's

TAP

Lightly taping a subject in various places is used frequently during hypnosis as a physical means of reinforcing suggestion. Also can be used in some confusion style inductions. The hypnotist stands behind the subject gently tapping them randomly about the shoulders and back of the head.

TERMINATION

This is the point at which we end the trance state and bring the subject back to a waking state. Also we can refer to the end of a session or even to end the course of treatment.

TEST

Tests are used to determine suggestibility see suggestibility tests. often referred to as exercises in order to avoid the idea of failure for the subject, this of course would be counterproductive consequence of reversed effect.They are also used once a subject is in trance in order to gauge the depth of hypnosis which has been achieved.

THERAPY

The treatment of illnesses and disorders

THETA

A state of meditative sleep where brainwave cycles are between 4 and 7.5 Hz

THOUGHT STOPPING

Used in order to stop intrusive destructive thoughts. The subject shouts the word stop internally and visualises a stop sign. Then makes a deliberate effort to change the pattern of thinking or the subject matter.

TIMELINE THERAPY

Using the time line forward as well as backward to make positive change and see the changes before they've been made.

TIME DISTORTION

A common hypnotic phenomena whereby the subject is unaware of time passing, this can be exaggerated to help prove hypnosis has taken place. A good convincer for some types of subjects.

TRANCE

One definition of the hypnotic state.

TRANSFERENCE

The process of emotional attachment of the subject to the hypnotist. This may come about due to the feelings of rapport between the two. As well as the rapport bond another deeper bond may begin to exist because of the successful treatment delivered by the hypnotist.

TRANSPOSITION

The changing of the sequence of events in a timeline when relating to a memory.

TRAUMA

An unpleasant event in a perons life, these can range from fairly minor like a dog barking and startling a small child to being emotionally or physically abused. It is the repression of these traumas which cause symptoms such as phobias, anxieties etc.

TREMORS

Sometimes witnessed in subjects in the deeper stages of trance. Small movements in the hand are one of the signs of trance. Also when using ideomotor response (finger signalling) trembling can often be seen.

TRIGGER

This is the input experienced by the subject which causes a symptom. An example would be that upon seeing a spider the subject has a phobic reaction. Triggers can also be used positively. The hypnotist may embed a positive reactiotoby using a post hypnotic suggestion to any trigger. Example; from this day forward every time you see the colour red it will serve as a powerful reminder to your sobconscious that you are a non smoker. For comedy a post hypnotic suggestion that whenever the hypnotist coughs the subject will shout 'peanuts' at the top of their voice.

We can also use a trigger to instigate anything we want during trance, for the subject to follow the sugestion,. When I click my fingers you will close your eyes. Used as part of a deepener. When I say the word easy you will go deeper relaxed.

TRY

A wonderful power word when used under the right circumstances the hypnotist invokes the law of reversed effect. By saying the word try you are implying that failure is not only real possibility but inevitable, due to our failures of willpower in the past.

Try to open your eyes you cannot...

In fact the harder you try...

The harder it is...

The more you try to open those eyes...

The harder it becomes...

They just stick tighter and tighter...

The harder you try.

TWENTY EIGHT DAYS

It is said by some that this is the period of time, one lunar cycle, that it takes to permanently change a habit.

THE U's and V's

UNCONSCIOUS

The part of the mind which deals with keepirg us alive it controls all of our involuntary functions like breathing. It is also responsible for our ancestral self preservation reactions, often called limbic reaction. These are the instinctive reactions we have to situations, these limbic reactions display themselves non verbally in our body language and facial expressions. These are the Fright Freeze Flight and Fight.

UP

This is the direction we should infer when emerging the subject. Also our voice should move upwards emotionally.

VAGUE

We should be vague with our language during inductions, especially in the early stages. It allows the subject some lateral movement in their interpretation of what is expected this is certainly true with nervous subjects. If we are too specific in our descriptions the suggestion may not be readily accepted which may lead eventually to rejection of subsequent suggestions. The effect of this can mean that in future the critical factor remains on high alert whenever the subject is in your presence. Even if the subject is consciously willing, hypnotising them may become a challenge.

VISUAL ACCESSING CUES

Observing eye movements to determine how a person relates to the world around them.

Looking left means they are thinking logically and to the right they are imagining. Up indicates a visual thinker to the side would indicate an auditory thinking and looking down indicates a kinesthetic.

VISUALISATION

Being able to mentally see an image, hence imagination

A hypnotic technique used for induction, deepeners and scripts. The subject is guided through the various processes using imagination and very vivid imagery. Appealing to all senses at the same time in order for the subject to really experience whatever scene is being set for them.

VISUAL TYPES

Someone who thinks in terms of images. They use their minds eye. They might reply to a statement made to them something like 'yes I can see what you are saying'

VOICE PATTERNS

Pertains to anything concerning how you use your voice during hypnosis. Inflection, cadence, depth included.

VOLUNTEER

A person putting themselves forward as a potential subject, usually for a stage performance.

THE W's

WAKING

Refers to either the process of waking up from either a natural or hypnotic sleep or being awake.

WAKING HYPNOSIS

State of suggestibility in which the attention is focused. Waking hypnosis takes place during seemingly normal conversation.

WAKING SUGGESTION

Suggestions made to a subject whilst they are awake or not hypnotised. whenever the subject is in the presence of the hypnotist he should take the opportunity to use suggestion, at least to lay seeds for the future. You can use waking suggestions to create the all important expectancy and belief as well as initial convinces. During a pretalk most of the information given to a a subject should be at least suggestive.

WELL BEING

This is the paramount objective of any hypnotist. The subject whether a client in a therapy room or a volunteer on stage has entrusted you with themselves, looking after them is the first consideration.

WHENEVER

Used as part of a trigger. Can be used in hypnotic and post hypnotic suggestion.Whenever you hear a certain price of music you will dance like Mick Jagger.

WHO CAN BE HYPNOTISED

Almost anyone can be hypnotised. The exceptions are the clinically insane and anyone unable to understand the instructions being given. Some take time and others can a achieve trance very quickly. Different individuals need different induction styles too.

Good pre talks. Assessments and susceptibility testing is needed to determine the best route.

WIDE AWAKE

This obviously refers to be in the waking state. As hypnotists we may sometimes use this statement in the contrary, especially for the entertainer. A stage hypnotist will often say ' eyes open wide awake' during a show. The subject actually remains in trance but their eyes open giving the appearance that they are indeed awake. Adds to the effect when they very out ridiculous suggestions.

In therapy it may be used during fraction is at I on. And of course as the final stage of emergence.

WILL POWER

This is the term we use when referring to doing something consciously. It is also one of the misconceptions attached to hypnosis that only people of weak or no will power can be hypnotised. Often will power can be our own worse enemy. We try to achieve a goal such as giving up zsmoking, we make a conscious effort and fail due to power of the subconscious, when that failure occurs it instills negative attitude. The subconscious now has preconceptions regarding failure when we attempt to use will power, so the next time we try to achieve a goal by conscious effort or will power we are doomed to fail. This is a vicious circle and starts at a very early age for most individuals. It is why we should never 'try' to do something we are preconditioned to fail due to our previous failures.

THE X, Y, Z

X RAY SPECS

An absolute must in any comedic hypnosis routine. Exactly as it sound the Wearer has xray vision. A great hallucination sketch goes something like this.

I'm going to give you a pair of spectacles. These are very special and expensive spectacles. Developed by NASA for astronaughts with special lenses. The lenses are made from xray material. Who ever puts on are spectacles can see through clothes. Whoever has thes spectacles on can see anyone they look at naked. When you open your eyes you will see that I am holding these spectacles. And if you were to wear them you too would see people as if naked....nod your head when you understand.

YES STATEMENTS

Statements often presented as questions made specifically to the subject to elicit a 'yes' answer from the recipient. A well known sales technique, the sales person asks a series of questions or makes seemingly inane comments and the potential client is compelled to agree. Once the salesman has the victim continually nodding he can move in with the half truths which will be more readily accepted. Politicians also do it. Tell you truism after truism then slip the lie in.

ZAP

A buzz word used in the entertainment industry meaning to hypnotise. Often people will referer to being zapped.

ZOMBIE

One of the classic signs of trance, the zombie or zombified look. Distant expression lethargic movements and relaxed features. Also one of the classic misconceptions that hypnotists can make a subject into a zombie completely under their power and influence.

If you have enjoyed this book please take the time to give an honest review. Perhaps you would also benefit from reading my other book

How to Hypnotise Stage, Street and Therapy

If you have any thoughts with regard to additional information which you believe could be included then please drop me a line at steveleapbooks@gmail.com

Copyright

This book is dedicated to my wife
Georgina

&

Aaron, Adam, Aidan

My three sons

For supporting me throughout the writing of this book

Follow Steve Leap on twitter

@steveleap